O Cross of Christ

Pope Francis

LITURGICAL PRESS

Collegeville, Minnesota

www.litpress.org

Cover design by Monica Bokinskie.

Cover and interior illustrations by Deborah Luke.

ISBN 978-0-8146-4554-3   ISBN 978-0-8146-4579-6 (ebook)

Introduction

On the evening of Good Friday, March 25, 2016, Pope Francis presided over the Stations of the Cross in the Coliseum in Rome. Of course, the setting is a fitting and dramatic one, since many Christians suffered martyrdom there in the days of imperial Rome.

The practice of the pope leading the Good Friday Stations there was begun by Pope Benedict XIV in the mid-1700s. The tradition was abandoned for a long time, until Pope Paul VI revived it in 1964, and it has been continued by his successors. These days, the prayerful event is followed annually by millions of people around the world by television and social media.

Typically, the pope invites a particular bishop or theologian to prepare original stational reflections each year. For 2016, the honor went to Cardinal Gualtiero Bassetti of Perugia, Italy. As Cardinal Bassetti's beautiful prayers were recited, people from various nations— including Syria, China, and the Central African Republic— carried a large cross from station to station.

But as the praying of the Stations came to a close, the Holy Father added a new and unexpected element. As the thousands of Romans and pilgrims who were present stood, holding lighted candles, Francis recited the text of an original prayer that he had composed, titled "O Cross of Christ." It prompts us to recognize Jesus' cross in a series of contemporary circumstances and people, first in several negative ones and then in several that are positive. That is the prayer presented in this booklet.

With the Vatican's permission, we have included a responsory line after each stanza of the prayer, in order to make it more conducive to prayer in a group setting. We also commissioned the original art you see included on these pages, by the American artist Deborah Luke.

In this useful booklet format, we recommend this prayer for use among families, youth groups, adult prayer groups, or parishes, especially during Lent.

Help us to recognize you, O Cross of Christ!

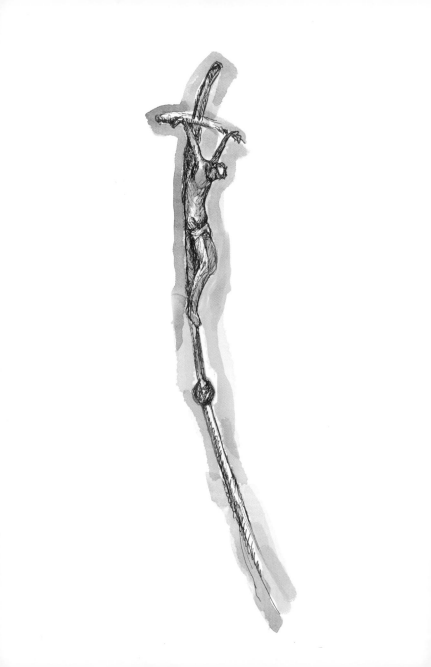

O Cross of Christ,

You are the symbol of divine love and of human injustice,
icon of the supreme sacrifice for love and of boundless
   selfishness even unto madness,
instrument of death and the way of resurrection,
sign of obedience and emblem of betrayal,
the gallows of persecution and the banner of victory.

Response: Save us, O Cross of Christ.

O Cross of Christ,

today too we see you raised up
in our sisters and brothers killed, burned alive,
throats slit and decapitated
by barbarous blades amid cowardly silence.

Response: Help us to recognize you, O Cross of Christ.

O Cross of Christ,

today too we see you in the faces of children,
of women and people, worn out and fearful,
who flee from war and violence
and who often only find death and many Pilates who wash
    their hands.

Response: Help us to recognize you, O Cross of Christ.

O Cross of Christ,

today too we see you in those filled with knowledge and not
    with the spirit,
scholars of death and not of life,
who instead of teaching mercy and life,
threaten with punishment and death,
and who condemn the just.

Response: Help us to recognize you, O Cross of Christ.

O Cross of Christ,

today too we see you in unfaithful ministers
who, instead of stripping themselves of their own vain
    ambitions,
divest even the innocent of their dignity.

Response: Help us to recognize you, O Cross of Christ.

O Cross of Christ,

today too we see you in the hardened hearts
of those who easily judge others,
with hearts ready to condemn even to the point of stoning,
without ever recognizing their own sins and faults.

Response: Help us to recognize you, O Cross of Christ.

O Cross of Christ,

today too we see you in expressions of fundamentalism
and in terrorist acts committed by followers of some
    religions
which profane the name of God
and which use the holy name to justify their unprecedented
    violence.

Response: Help us to recognize you, O Cross of Christ.

O Cross of Christ,

today too we see you in those who wish to remove you
from public places and exclude you from public life,
in the name of a pagan laicism
or that equality you yourself taught us.

Response: Help us to recognize you, O Cross of Christ.

O Cross of Christ,

today too we see you in the powerful and in arms dealers
who feed the cauldron of war
with the innocent blood of our brothers and sisters,
and give their children blood-soaked bread to eat.

Response: Help us to recognize you, O Cross of Christ.

O Cross of Christ,

today too we see you in traitors
who, for thirty pieces of silver,
would consign anyone to death.

Response: Help us to recognize you, O Cross of Christ.

O Cross of Christ,

today too we see you in thieves and corrupt officials
who, instead of safeguarding the common good and morals,
sell themselves in the despicable marketplace of immorality.

Response: Help us to recognize you, O Cross of Christ.

O Cross of Christ,

today too we see you in the foolish
who build warehouses to store up treasures that perish,
leaving Lazarus to die of hunger at their doorsteps.

Response: Help us to recognize you, O Cross of Christ.

O Cross of Christ,

today too we see you in the destroyers of our "common home,"
who by their selfishness ruin the future of coming generations.

Response: Help us to recognize you, O Cross of Christ.

O Cross of Christ,

today too we see you in the elderly
who have been abandoned by their families,
in the disabled and in children starving and cast off
by our egotistical and hypocritical society.

Response: Help us to recognize you, O Cross of Christ.

O Cross of Christ,

today too we see you in the Mediterranean and Aegean Seas
which have become insatiable cemeteries,
reflections of our indifferent and anesthetized conscience.

Response: Help us to recognize you, O Cross of Christ.

O Cross of Christ,

image of love without end and way of the Resurrection,
today too we see you in noble and upright persons
who do good without seeking praise or admiration from
    others.

Response: Help us to recognize you, O Cross of Christ.

O Cross of Christ,

we, too, see you in ministers who are faithful and humble,
who illuminate the darkness of our lives
like candles that burn freely
in order to brighten the lives of the least among us.

Response: Help us to recognize you, O Cross of Christ.

O Cross of Christ,

today too we see you in the faces of consecrated women
    and men
—good Samaritans—
who have left everything to bind up, in evangelical silence,
the wounds of poverty and injustice.

Response: Help us to recognize you, O Cross of Christ.

O Cross of Christ,

today too we see you in the merciful
who have found in mercy the greatest expression of justice
 and faith.

Response: Help us to recognize you, O Cross of Christ.

O Cross of Christ,

today too we see you in simple men and women
who live their faith joyfully day in and day out,
in filial observance of your commandments.

Response: Help us to recognize you, O Cross of Christ.

O Cross of Christ,

today too we see you in the contrite,
who in the depths of the misery of their sins,
are able to cry out:
Lord, remember me in your kingdom!

Response: Help us to recognize you, O Cross of Christ.

O Cross of Christ,

we, too, see you in the blessed and the saints
who know how to cross the dark night of faith
without ever losing trust in you
and without claiming to understand your mysterious
    silence.

Response: Help us to recognize you, O Cross of Christ.

O Cross of Christ,

today too we see you in families
that live their vocation of married life
in fidelity and fruitfulness.

Response: Help us to recognize you, O Cross of Christ.

O Cross of Christ,

today too we see you in volunteers
who generously assist those in need and the downtrodden.

Response: Help us to recognize you, O Cross of Christ.

O Cross of Christ,

today too we see you in those persecuted for their faith
who, amid their suffering,
continue to offer an authentic witness
to Jesus and the Gospel.

Response: Help us to recognize you, O Cross of Christ.

O Cross of Christ,

today too we see you in those who dream,
those with the heart of a child,
who work to make the world a better place,
ever more human and just.

Response: Help us to recognize you, O Cross of Christ.

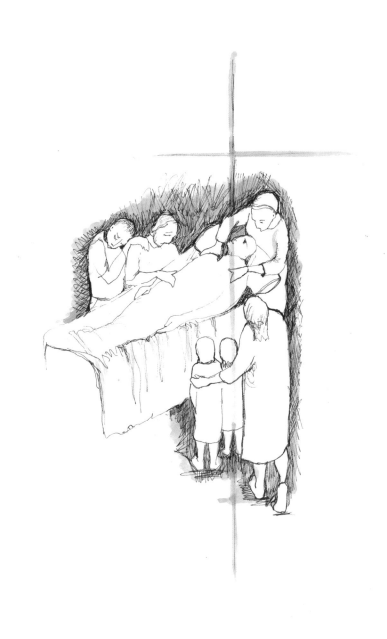

In you, Holy Cross,
we see God who loves even to the end,
and we see the hatred of those who want to dominate,
that hatred which blinds the minds and hearts
of those who prefer darkness to light.

Response: Save us, O Cross of Christ.

O Cross of Christ,
Ark of Noah that saved humanity from the flood of sin,
save us from evil and from the Evil One.

Response: Save us, O Cross of Christ.

O Throne of David
and seal of the divine and eternal Covenant,
awaken us from the seduction of vanity!
O cry of love, inspire in us a desire for God, for goodness
    and for light.

Response: Save us, O Cross of Christ.

O Cross of Christ,

teach us that the rising of the sun
is more powerful than the darkness of night.
O Cross of Christ,
teach us that the apparent victory of evil
vanishes before the empty tomb
and before the certainty of the Resurrection
and the love of God
which nothing can defeat, obscure, or weaken.

Response: Amen!

About the Artist

Deborah Luke's journey as an artist began in 1971 at Dominican College in New Orleans. There she studied with noted Louisiana sculptor Angela Gregory who studied under Antoine Bourdelle, considered one of the most accomplished students of Auguste Rodin. Forty years later, Luke's work can be found in private homes, hospitals, schools, and churches throughout the United States.

Since 1996, her work has centered on the life and passion of Christ. She welcomes the challenge of bringing to life works inspired by holy Scripture and informed by the needs of worshiping communities. Deborah is an artist member of the Association of Consultants for Liturgical Space.